I0070940

Salespeople Are Like Tacos
The Real Reasons You Are Losing Sales You Should Win

by

Richard Grehalva

Author of:
Unleashing the Power
Of
Consultative Selling

Salespeople Are Like Tacos

Copyright © 2018 by Richard Grehalva

All rights reserved, including the right of reproduction, in whole or in part, in any form, without the express written permission of the author.

Published by: P2P People to People Communications Media

Sales/Marketing

ISBN: 0-9763818-5-0

Paperback

www.resultsnotadvice.com

Contents

Introduction

In 2004 my book unleashing the Power of Consultative Selling: Selling the Way your Customer Wants to Buy… Not the Way You Like to Sell was published. The book was based on my experiences from leading a sales and marketing team and from my sales training programs.

Here's the thing: I developed my sales program not by design, but out of necessity. Let me explain.

The backstory is that I had moved into leading a sales and marketing team from my role in leading an operations group. I quickly found that each person followed their own process for selling. This was unlike operations, which follows a process yet allows flexibility in meeting the end objective.

I decided to get sales training for the group, and as I investigated what was available, I found that it was outdated and ineffective in a quickly changing market. What was happening was one of the most significant events of our time – the internet. The sales trainings offered then were stuck in the past and did not represent what salespeople actually did; and most were silent about the internet.

I decided to develop my own system. Not because it would take me to where it has, but because to succeed meant to move away from what was being offered and to create a methodology to become a high-performance sales team.

Once again, I found myself in the same place as I did before. The majority of sales training being offered today has not kept pace with today's massively informed buyer.

In sales you're either a taco, taquito or enchilada. It's basically all the same stuff with a different price point and presentation. The number one issue facing salespeople is differentiating themselves from their competition. "Salespeople are Like Tacos: The Real Reason Why You're Losing Sales You Should Win" describes who your real competitor you are ignoring. The old ways of selling no longer work. Learn what it takes to crush your quota and make your competition irrelevant.

B2B and B2C is a myth. Businesses and Consumers do not buy –People buy. Today it is People to People selling. It means understanding how people decide to buy and how to position yourself to win more than you lose.

The most important thing in sales is quota. Everyone is measured on it, from the CEO to the individual salesperson, yet 7 out 10 of salespeople will miss their quota. The real measurement is not quota, it is sales productivity.

The information and processes needed to lead and coach a sales team that crushes quota quarter after quarter are not simple accidents. The book represents not theory but actual day-to-day experience in my role as a CEO of two companies. I'm the CEO of both a consulting company and a sales and marketing transformation firm. These roles give me a ringside seat to observation of what works and what does not work.

At the back of this book I offer you a list of both free and paid resources to help you pursue your decision to change from what you are doing now to something different in order to achieve a different outcome – because when you change your mindset, you will change your results.

All the best and happy selling,

Rich Grehalva

Chapter 1
Salespeople Are Like Tacos

I was at one time a senior vice-president of global sales and marketing for a company in India. A few team members came to the United States from India to meet with me. I took them to a Mexican restaurant for lunch. Now if you haven't been to India I can tell you I never saw a Mexican restaurant all the times I went there and I went to India often.

They were looking at the menu and I asked me what was a taco?

I told them it was a deep-fried corn tortilla folded stuffed with your choice of chicken or beef served with lettuce, tomatoes, cheese and sour cream. Then they asked what is an enchilada? I told them it was a lightly-fried corn tortilla loosely folded stuffed with your choice of chicken or beef served with lettuce, tomatoes, cheese and sour cream. They then asked, "What about the taquito? I told them it was a deep-fried corn tortilla tightly folded stuffed with your choice of chicken or beef served with lettuce, tomatoes, cheese and sour cream. Basically, the same stuff with a different presentation and price point. This is what salespeople are like. They cannot really effectively communicate their value.

They struggle in attempting to show why they are different from their competitors yet fail at doing this. They all sound the same just a different presentation of the same basic stuff with a different price point. Just like how I answered the question about tacos.

What does this have to do with selling?

89% of salespeople fail at executive conversations according to Sirius Decisions. Why is this? Because they do not provide insights. They ask questions that prospects and clients roll their eyes when they hear it. What is the question? What keeps you up at night? They know the salesperson will turn this around and try to sell them something from what they told them.

What do they want? They want you to tell them something they don't know not what they already know. When a prospect or client says "I didn't know that?" This is an insight. They know you have knowledge they don't because you get to speak and sell to a number of people in their market and want you to use what you know to help them.

Telling me smoking was bad for my health or I would die was not enough. I knew that. What I didn't know was how I connected my emotions to cigarettes and where the source of these emotions came from. This was the difference that made a difference.

The question isn't "What keeps you up at night?" The question is "This is what should keep you up at night?" This is an insight and it means you must research your client's or prospects business to uncover what that might be and this will separate you from the rest of the salespeople who will ask "What keeps you up at night?"

What are you really selling?

I ask this question of my own sales teams as well as the ones that attend my trainings. How would you answer my question of "what do you sell?"

How do they answer the question? The same way as everyone else by using a canned elevator speech?

What is the real answer?
Change

Everything we are asking our client to do comes down to this. We are asking them:

- To change from one vendor to another.
- Change what they have not been doing to something different.
- You may be asking them to change their workforce to new way of doing things.
- You may even be asking them to change by taking a risk on achieving a better outcome.

In every chapter of this book I'm inviting you to change from what you are doing now to something different.

Here is what I know about selling *"you are selling change"* and *"people don't like change."*

How many things do you know about yourself you should change? Knowing the change will bring you more money, improve a relationship, advance your career, create joy in your life and the list goes on. Yet, if you know the change will improve your life why don't you do it? Or better yet *"Why haven't you done already?"*

Guess what if you won't change what makes you think your client will?

Why don't we make these changes? Because bad feels good and good feels bad. I use to have a terrible smoking habit and I knew it was bad for me. I knew it could cause cancer. No matter how many times I was told or heard it I would not quit. Even though I knew if I did it would be a healthy choice and I would live longer.

Why didn't I stop? Because even when I thought about it or even when I tried to stop smoking I went back and grabbed another cigarette. Why because making the change was hard and *"good felt bad."* *"Bad felt Good"* and smoking was my comfort zone even though I knew it would affect my health.

When did I stop? I woke up one morning with what felt like I had a smoking hangover. It was then that I got sacred. I knew smoking was no longer safe and bad no longer felt good, it felt bad.

This was the first day of making the changes to stop smoking and yes it was the hardest thing I ever had to do. Change was difficult and hard however the reward was worth it.

How does choice affect selling?

I knew without people telling me quitting smoking that I would live longer. Smoking or not smoking was not a choice it was a dilemma. I was screwed if I did and I was screwed If I didn't. Choosing between two things is not a choice. It will always create problems and what we usually do is nothing. We just decide not to decide by staying where we are at and this is a decision.

58% of deals end up stalled in the pipeline ending up with no decision. Why is this? Salespeople are selling choice:

- Choose me not them.
- Use my product or service not theirs.

Is this really a choice? Pick "this or that" or pick "me and not them" is not a choice. It is a dilemma.

Why people do what they do?

We are not selling to an industry, market or job titles. We are people selling to people. This is why no matter how good your product or service is it will not sell itself. Selling and marketing encompasses two important things human behavior and math.

Sales processes fail to include this in their programs. Instead the focus is on features and benefits, closing techniques, competition, pricing these are all aspects of *"buy from me"*, *"not from them."* I'm not suggesting you ignore this however what I'm strongly suggesting is to incorporate how to sell to people.

Consider this: relationships are discussed as one of the most important aspects of gaining and retaining clients yet understanding how we as humans decide is not taught or coached by sales leaders and is missing from sales processes and training programs.

Worse yet, salespeople and sales leaders fail to identify their greatest competitor. Who is it? It is not another company it is "no decision" and 58% of deals are stopped in the pipeline. Salespeople and sales leaders are losing deals they should have won as a result of not understanding how to develop a strategy to turn "no deal" to a "deal."

Why do we decide to do nothing? Because of something called "The Status Quo Bias." This comes from Behavioral Economics that combines economics and psychology to explain why people make certain decisions and choices, including purchasing decisions, and how we can use this understanding to change behavior.

Several psychologists and behavioral economists have identified the cause or causes of the bias. The evidence shows the status quo bias is caused by a number of other biases in decision making. The following is what the experts tell us:

- Daniel Kahneman says status quo bias is related to loss aversion. He points to that most people make the status quo their reference point and tend to view change from the status quo as a loss. Because we perceive and weigh losses greater than potential gains, we become loss averse, which makes us inclined to stay with the status quo.

- Richard Thaler believes the status quo bias results from a psychological phenomenon called the endowment effect, which refers to the fact that most people like and value something more simply because they already own it. The endowment effect causes us to overvalue the benefits of the status quo and to under-appreciate its disadvantages.

- Some psychologists attribute status quo bias to a human desire to avoid or delay difficult or complicated choices, and there is evidence showing that people are more likely to stick with the status quo when the alternatives are difficult to evaluate or compare.

So how can marketing and sales professionals combat the status quo bias? Because the status quo bias is inherently non-rational, there are no silver-bullet solutions. Yet, once you understand how we decide it allows you to increase your ability to win by speaking and presenting in ways that are more effective.

What to do next?

B2B and B2C is a myth. Businesses do not sell to businesses and businesses do not sell to consumers. We are P2P people selling to people. You must update your selling mindset by understanding to win more is not just presenting your product or service to demonstrate why you are different from your competitor. It is understanding we are asking and selling change and we do not like to change. And the real competitor is the status quo bias because this is the source of a client making a no decision.

What is getting in the way? It's the ability or inability for salespeople to articulate value. Most products are good enough says Simon Hayward of Gartner. The problem is how to differentiate one company over another. 80% of salespeople focus too much on their product and service according to buyers from research conducted by Forrester Research.

Salespeople in their pitch often say to their clients and prospects their product or service provides value. In my training workshops, I ask salespeople to define value. This becomes difficult for them to answer and usually it goes back to some version of the canned elevator pitch.

I discovered a formula earlier for selling which is $P+R=S$ problem plus result equals solution. What's the point of offering a solution if you don't know what the problem is or the result? This is the first step to help us define value.

What is value from the byers perspective? There is the formula for this as well. It is based on my own research to answer the question of value. $V=R-P$ value equals result minus problem. Value defined by clients is really simple. Once they get the results they wanted and the problem has been eliminated this is how they measure value.

What moves us to change? Staying in our comfort zone is going to become uncomfortable.

Knowing we really sell change and understanding the status quo needs to be defeated to win more means you must change. You are at a crossroad right now. You are looking at the dilemma to stay where you are at or make a change in the way you sell. We also know you probably will do what most do when facing the crossroad-nothing.

I do not want this for you. I want to offer you choice more than that flexibility. This is what I'll cover in the next chapter ***"Using your Brain for a Change"***.

Chapter 2
Using Your Brain for a Change

Selling to people logically is not logical. White papers and case studies all make sense, and this is the problem. Ever hear the expression **"People buy on emotion and justify with logic"?** Well, there is truth to this.

Salespeople and marketing professionals communicate their products and services in ways so clients can think in well-reasoned, linear ways as they evaluate them. The problem is, they don't think this way.

One example is buying a car. People do not consciously assess a car's benefits feature by feature and decide whether to buy it. Instead, they buy from their emotions, like the want for happiness, prestige, and so on. These play a bigger role than logic in the purchase decision.

In preparing presentations, salespeople believe clients can explain their thinking and behavior. In reality, 95% of thinking takes place in our unconscious minds. People use conscious thought primarily as a way to rationalize behavior.

Salespeople think that having the best pitch with the right words is all you need to win. Yet brain scans suggest that only a small portion of the brain's neural activity ultimately surfaces in language.

This is based on the research done for How Customers Think by Gerald Zaltman.

You really need to understand what is going on in our minds to be able to effectively communicate to a client or prospect. This begins by finding out about the brain and its three parts.

The **"new brain"** thinks logically. The new brain is the last to evolve. The neocortex is credited with the development of human language, abstract thought, imagination, and consciousness. It includes the two large cerebral hemispheres and has almost infinite learning abilities.

The *"middle brain"* feels emotions. The middle brain is like the information highway between the other two parts of the brain. This is the part of your brain that records memories of behaviors that produced pleasant or unpleasant experiences. It's responsible for your emotions and value judgments.

The *"old brain"* decides and pushes the action button. Seth Godin refers to the oldest part of the brain as the "lizard brain." Remember that the reptilian brain is primitive. It's not concerned with gaining pleasure; it's concerned with avoiding pain. The old brain quickly views situations to determine if you are at risk or danger. This is the "fight or flight" reaction.

Why is this important to know? Because in selling and marketing you are first selling to the lizard brain, and this part of the brain has no language. Typically, salespeople attempt to sell to the new brain, and this is what prompts clients to not decide, resulting in what salespeople refer to as a *"stalled deal."*

Neuromarketing proves that clients and prospects are like you and I are all human. A salesperson's target buyers make decisions to change and buy based on emotion, while justifying with facts. Neuromarketing, a concept developed by psychologists at Harvard University in 1990, is a field of marketing research that examines consumers' sensorimotor, cognitive, and affective responses to marketing stimuli.

Patrick Renvoisé and Christophe Morin wrote a book called Neuromarketing and they offer a framework for marketing and selling to the old brain. It consists of *"the only six stimuli that speak to the old brain."* The six triggers are:

1. Self-centeredness
2. Contrast
3. Tangible input
4. The beginning and the end
5. Visual stimuli
6. Emotion

18

How do you use this information about neuromarketing to improve the way you sell? Here are easy ways to remember how to stimulate our old lizard brain.

ME–Many of you may have heard someone say, **"WIIFM,"** meaning, **"What's In It For Me."** The old brain is self-centered and cares about its own survival. It's not worried about anybody else's survival. One of the ways the old brain views other people is, **"are you with me or against me?"**

Use the word **"You,"** not **"We"** or **"Me."**

SEE -Vision is our dominant sense, and the old brain responds most strongly to it. Research estimates that 80 to 85% of our perception, learning, cognition, and activities are mediated through vision.

Use pictures and props to show what you are talking about.

FEEL –Do you remember your first kiss, your wedding day, the birth of your child, the Challenger tragedy? Emotion helps the old brain to find things that are important to be remembered. Do you remember the meetings you had last year or what you had for lunch last week? These types of events are easy to forget, unless an emotion is tied to it.

Use stories as a way of bringing emotion to your presentations and conversations.

TOUCH –Imagining that you can increase your productivity or get more money is not what the old brain responds to. It must be something that you could touch, and the language you use must convey this to the old brain.

Use pictures to break down a complex idea to simple benefit-and-use language that turns **"imagine"** into to something concrete.

THIS or THAT -The old brain struggles without contrast. And the more similar the things being contrasted in your messaging are, the more powerful the impact will be. The contrast shows your clients and prospects why staying in their comfort zone (where they are now) is actually uncomfortable, and they need to move to a different solution.

Use a *"this"* strategy describing what happens if you stay in your comfort zone and the "that" of what happens when you get the outcome you want. Remember, value is when your problem has been eliminated and you get the measurable result you wanted.

START and FINISH –What movie is the line "a long time ago in a galaxy far, far away" from? Star Wars, of course. How about this one – "Louis, I think this is the beginning of a beautiful friendship"? Casablanca, the classic starring Humphrey Bogart. Your old brain is influenced by beginnings and endings and is on alert for the unexpected.

Use a *"pattern interrupt"* in the beginning of your presentation by saying or showing something your client or prospect is not expecting – meaning, something the old brain is not used to hearing. Remember when I said *"Salespeople are like tacos"?* I bet you recall that, because you weren't expecting to hear it.

So, what are the three mistakes salespeople make?

Mistake #1: Creating presentations and conversations designed for the logical new brain. So, now you know your reptilian brain makes the irrational decisions. Since rational decisions are so difficult to make, your reptilian brain is very important.

If your product or service is not the rationally best choice, you must appeal to the lizard brain. If you appeal to the new brain, it will analyze the facts and determine that you're not the best choice. Here's the secret: our products and services may not be the most rational choice.

If your product is the rationally the best choice, you must appeal to the lizard brain. The new brain will then come into play as your new brain has done a lot of critical thinking; yet the lizard brain will be the decision-maker, so you need to optimize in favor of it.

Mistake #2: Selling benefits and outcomes. You've heard that finding the *"pain"* is important in selling, yet salespeople sell outcomes. They talk about benefits and what you will get, not what you will lose.

This is the opposite of what the mind will do. We are two to three times more likely to make a decision to avoid a loss than we are to make a decision to gain something, according to the *"prospect theory."*

This theory was the conclusion reached by behavior economists Daniel Kahneman and Amos Tversky, who tested the concepts of loss aversion. Loss aversion is our resistance to losing what we have. Risk seeking, on the other hand, is our willingness to take risks.

Mistake #3: Not aligning your sales process with how customers buy. When I wrote my first book, Unleashing the Power of Consultative Selling, I based it on my experiences leading a sales and marketing team. I was moved from an operations position to leading the sales organization. I wanted to get my new team sales training after discovering that every one of the salespeople had their own system for selling.

What I found was that the sales training at the time was outdated, ineffective, and did not reflect what salespeople actually did in their day-to-day role. So, I created my own system out of necessity. The program was so successful that I launched my own sales and marketing training consulting business. I never started out to do this – it came out of my observation of what the best salespeople (versus the rest of them) were doing and my desire to gather and replicate what I learned.

The most important decision we make as salespeople, managers, and leaders is how to connect with our customers, clients, and prospects. They expect a perspective, an insight, not a sales pitch. This is why my subtitle for my book about sales training was "Selling the Way Your Customer Wants to Buy… Not the Way You Like to Sell." This is what I discovered the top salespeople were doing differently from all the rest.

Clients and prospects don't need your product or services. They do not wake up thinking, "if I only had your product or service, all my problems would be gone." If they make a decision to buy your product or service, it is not to solve your problem of making quota. It is to solve a business problem; their need is rarely met solely by buying a single product or stand-alone solution. The product or service you're offering is part of the total solution.

Here is an example of what is happening every week and may be happening to you. You review your sales pipeline funnel and you see a stuck opportunity. At every review of the sales funnel, the update is the closing date being pushed out. There are many excuses for this reality, but the status is the same: the opportunity is stuck. Does this sound painfully familiar?

In your review of the sales process steps, you can see that you or the salesperson completed everything; it's now a decision you are waiting on from the prospect. Everything's done on your side.

The salesperson forecasts the opportunity and projects a close date. However, that salesperson followed his sales process, which was not aligned with the client's buying process. The prospect isn't yet certain of the need to change, or change now, but the salesperson is certain it is time to close because, from his standpoint, he has done everything which his process dictates that he should do.

What to do next?

The selling mindset is the focus of this book; however, equally important is the buyer mindset. Most important of all, however, is that we remember we're not just sellers or buyers. It is not "us" selling to "them." This type of thinking is, as you now know, a dilemma. A more accurate description is *"people communicating with people."*

Think about a people-to-people selling mindset this way: we all have problems and we want to solve them. You seek help from people you know, like, and trust. Think about the people you go to for honest advice. You seek out people who have experience, knowledge, and information to provide you with what is needed to solve your issues.

This is the type of person your prospects and clients will see you as if you work on your selling mindset. Not as someone just trying to sell them something, but rather as the person who can help them overcome obstacles to get to the result they are after. This is the mindset of top performers, and this is what separates them from the rest.

Do you think your prospect and client meetings are productive?

The problem is not that salespeople don't know how to deliver a sales pitch; but where they find difficulty is in having a conversation. Are the first slides in your presentation all about how big your company is, how many locations you have, and how many logos of clients flash by on the screen, followed by all your services and products? Isn't it no wonder that clients answer on survey after survey that they view salespeople as not understanding them or their problem?

Too many times salespeople jump in telling prospects why their product or service is great and explaining the benefits of choosing them versus others. Selling to the new brain with logic. What can you do instead?

Live inside your client's world. Here's the thing: like you, they care about ways to improve their day-to-day lives. And there is no better method of appealing to this desire than an engaging story which moves your clients to a decision to buy because it "lives in their world" and speaks to their pain, obstacles, and fears, engaging the lizard brain instead of droning on about benefits and features of your product or service.

Chapter 3
The Conversion Conversation: Overcoming the "No Decision"

Status quo is really the number one competitor of salespeople. Deals which you think you lost over price are often in reality lost because the client decided to stay with the status quo. Moving from one product or service supplier to another is usually not a dilemma due to loving their current supplier all that much. They just don't want to go through the pain of making a change.

When having a conversion conversation, the status quo bias of clients must be "disrupted." In decision making, our brains are tuned to give negative impacts more weight than positive ones, and this is the root theory of status quo bias. Remember, "bad feels good" and ***good feels bad.***

Before we go further, let's do a brief recap:

- Our selling mindset is best described by Dan Sullivan: "Getting people intellectually engaged in a future result that's GOOD for THEM, and getting them to emotionally commit to take action to achieve that result."

- We are presenting to the lizard brain and there are six triggers: ME, SEE, FEEL, TOUCH, THIS or THAT, BEGINNING, and ENDING.

- We are two to three times more likely to make a decision to avoid a loss than they are to make a decision to attain a gain, according to something called the "prospect theory."

- We are selling change and people don't like change. The status quo bias "tells" you to stay in your current state because it means that you won't have to make a decision and therefore you can be sure there won't be any consequences of a bad decision.

If there is only one thing you remember from this book, then here is what it should be:

Before a client or prospect will buy your product or service, they first need to buy into the need for change, or you have no deal.

If you are doing any of the following in your presentations, it's time to stop getting in your own way of closing sales. Stop:

- Talking about you and your company.
- Talking about your product or service.
- Talking about features and benefits.
- Talking about the competition.
- Giving demos of your products.
- Giving white papers of your services.

These tactics, as you now know, are encouraging your prospect or client to stay where they are now. This is selling to the logical new brain, not to the lizard brain, and it keeps the prospect or client in their status quo.

Remember my struggle to quit smoking? Others telling me that smoking would kill me was all directed to my logical brain – and guess what? It did not work. I did not stop or change my habit.

It happened when my lizard brain woke up. I finally got to the point where I was no longer comfortable with the status quo. In my case, I was scared, so I changed to avoid the emotional pain.

85 to 90 percent of sales calls are perceived from prospects and clients as communicating no value. Sirius Decisions discovered that only 10 percent of executive's survey sales calls as providing enough value to justify the time spent on them. Forrester Research determined that only 15 percent of sales calls add enough value. No surprise, when salespeople have been told to sell benefits.

Expecting resistance to change from the start of your selling conversation will allow you to effectively manage objections.

It's not possible to be aware of all sources of resistance to change. Expecting that there will be resistance to change and being prepared to manage it is a proactive step. Recognizing behaviors that indicate possible resistance will raise awareness of the need to address the concerns. Here are some of the reactions to change:

Not understanding the need for change. When the reason for the change is unclear or if the prospect or client does not understand the need for change, you can expect resistance; especially if they strongly believe the current way of doing things works well.

Fear of the unknown. One of the most common reasons for resistance is fear of the unknown. People will only take action toward the unknown if they genuinely believe, and more importantly, feel, that the risks of staying where they are greater than those of moving forward in a new direction.

Lack of competence. People don't like to admit it but sometimes changing means learning new skills. Some people feel they won't be able to make the transition and will be judged for failing.

Connected to the old way. If you ask people to do things in a new way, as rational as that new way may seem to you, you will be setting yourself up against all their emotional connections to *"bad feels good."*

Poor communication. This is self- evident, isn't it? It's why clients and prospects continue to complain about the inability to have a conversation with salespeople about value.

Changes to routines. When we talk about comfort zones, we're really referring to routines. You and I love them. They make us feel safe and doing things differently is difficult.

Benefits and rewards. The benefits and rewards for making a change are often not seen as adequate for the trouble involved.

Change in the status quo. The perceptions of the change can make people feel they'll be worse off at the end of the change, and because of this, they are unlikely to give it their full support.

The prospect's status quo bias represents their natural tendency towards loss aversion. People stay where they are, even in an undesirable situation, because fear of loss is greater than hope for gain.

It doesn't appear there's a great deal of cost associated with doing nothing.

That needs to change. You must move from a presentation to a conversion conversation.

Earlier I asked you about the person you go to for advice. It's someone you know, like, and trust. Often these types of friends will come to you and offer an insight – something you personally were not aware of. They point out that if you do nothing, it will cause a problem in your life. They are not making a presentation. They are having a conversion conversation. They are helping you to move from your comfort zone because staying where you are at is no longer safe.

This must be your mindset in having a conversion conversation. And you have these types of conversations all the time. Here are a few examples:

- A conversation about going to see a movie you feel that both of you may enjoy.

- A conversation about going to a restaurant you like and you feel they may enjoy as well.

- A conversation about going to a vacation spot you like and you feel they should consider as well.

You also have conversion conversations on a serious note.

- A conversation with your children about going to a college which you feel may benefit their life.

- A conversation with a friend or a relative about changing a behavior which you believe is harmful to them, where you explain that you feel this change will improve their life.

Our selling mindset is best described by Dan Sullivan: "Getting people intellectually engaged in a future result that's GOOD for THEM, and getting them to emotionally commit to take action to achieve that result." Isn't this what a conversion conversation is, no matter where or why you are having it with someone?

28

How we decide NOT to decide

The first step in having a conversion conversation is understanding "how we decide not to decide."

Comfort Zone. We all have our comfort zone where things feel familiar and we are at ease and in control of our environment, experiencing low levels of anxiety and stress. In this zone, a steady level of performance is possible. It is a "sameness strategy," and this is what keeps you from deciding to take action.

Effort. We think about how much effort the change will take and whether it is really worth it. This is when "bad feels good."

WIIFM. What's In It For Me? You may have heard this expression before because it is true. We ponder the change, and if we can't see how we can benefit, we don't do it.

Confusion. The change being suggested is not all that different from what you are doing now. The contrast between where you are now and the future is not great enough to make the change.

What needs to happen is, using what you've just read, you need to defeat your real competitor –the status quo bias.

What to do next? Overcome Your Prospect's Status Quo Bias.

To overcome the status quo means disturbing it – otherwise, expect the same results, with 60% of decisions becoming stalled in the pipeline.

It takes 3 Yeses to Win.

Here's what to do to in a conversion conversation. You must understand that in order to win sales, you must not get one yes, you need to get three – and there is a correct order.

Yes #1 –Time for a change.

Unless your prospect or client agrees that it's time to change, you will have difficulty in getting a win. And this most likely will end up as a stalled deal in your pipeline. You must provide an insight that moves them from the comfort zone to the **"discomfort zone."** Quantify the cost for the client to keep the status quo. Bring up lost sales, higher costs, and so on. If you do not communicate the current situation in terms of creating a loss in money and/or time, the client's lizard brain will automatically opt to stay where he's at.

Pattern Interrupt. A pattern interrupt is a technique designed to change a particular thought, behavior, or situation. Your objective is to redirect the prospect's thoughts from what they were thinking to focus on the thing you are offering. What you are doing is basically interrupting the prospect's current pattern and redirecting them to your chosen path. **"Salespeople are like tacos"** is an example. My point was to show you how salespeople sound and look alike.

Loss. Understand the cost of **"nothing."** The problem is that we tend to think that doing nothing is better than doing something different. It's best to simply stay where we're at. It's called the endowment effect. This is the theory that people tend to ascribe more value to the things they already own.

In his book Why We Buy: The Science of Shopping, Paco Underhill suggests that "we esteem things more highly after we buy them." This is the endowment effect in action.

Putting these things together leads to a powerful recipe for not taking action.

- "My current situation is valuable to me."
- "I don't want to risk a bad outcome in my next decision."
- "What's the danger in staying put?"

Yes #2 – The time is now.

Once the prospect or client agrees that it's time for a change, the next step is getting them to agree that the time to take action is now. To do this means highlighting the impact of doing nothing.

What's at risk of doing nothing? This is when you must think about the prospect's lizard brain and how to communicate to it. If you want to overcome their status quo bias, you must counteract their strongly ingrained urge to stick with they know or what they are doing now. You must focus on what they will lose before telling them what they will gain.

Yes #3 – I'm the right guide.

Imagine you have decided to climb Mt. Everest. What will be one of the most important things you will consider?

Is it the equipment? Is it the cost?

Or is it: Will I be safe?

The third question is probably a big one in your mind. So, selecting your guide is going to be important. If you read all the marketing material, you might think:

Guides are like tacos. They all talk about getting you to the summit.

What if you read all the guides' marketing material and while interviewing them, each one told you their success record of getting their clients to the summit. How would you select one?

What if one guide began by saying, "Safety is our major concern. 12% of people who lose their lives doing this climb do so during the first and safest leg of the trip –going up. However, the most dangerous part of the climb is coming down, where 56% of people lose their lives. We focus on getting you down safely, to get you home"? Would this guide be your choice?

Path – You must be able to show a "path" for your prospect of client to take. They don't want to take the risk of making a mistake, and this is why they would rather choose doing nothing as the safest option. Show them a way that clearly separates you from your competitors. The best way to do this is to tell them a story of someone like them who took the proposed path and got the outcome they desired safely.

Connection – You have an emotional connection to people you like, know, and trust. To do that with your prospects and clients, it's helpful to connect to the very core of two critical principles of motivation:

- WIIFM – What's In It For Me? People buy to improve their lives.
- Move Away from Pain – The quicker they buy, the faster their lives improve.

If you lose money, you can make it up; however if you lose time, you can never go back and get it. Time is valuable. The longer you wait to move toward a better situation, the longer you live with your dissatisfaction.

Let me give another personal example. I used to be constantly tired and aggravated from poor sleep. My wife had to sleep with a pillow over her head due to my snoring. I was told to go see a sleep doctor but I chose to put it off. Why? For fear of having to wear a CPAP mask while I slept. Once again, the arguments I heard in favor of seeing the doctor appealed only to my logical new brain, which I of course ignored.

I have led men's retreats for over 20 years, and at one of them, one of the men on staff was a doctor. In the morning, he said to me, "Rich, I'm scared for you. Do you realize how many times you stopped breathing last night when you were sleeping?" He said to me, "You have sleep apnea and need to get a sleep study done." I really did not know I was not breathing during my unrestful sleep. This was an insight. What did I do? Nothing, until Reggie White, the former football great, died in his sleep from – you guessed it – sleep apnea.

I went to get a sleep study done and got my CPAP machine and mask. The first thing I said to my wife was: *"So, this is what it feels like to sleep all night!"* After all this, I told her I wished I had taken those steps a long time ago.

How many examples similar to my own do you have? Logical doesn't work to the illogical mind. Talking sense is nonsense to the lizard brain. Often it is an insight into something you didn't know that wakes up the lizard brain to be open to change.

32

To beat your number competitor, status quo bias, you must incorporate *"The 3 Yeses Strategy"* to get a win.

Yes #1 – Time for a change.

Yes #2 – The time is now.

Yes #3 – I'm the right guide.

Do this and you will make your competition irrelevant.

Chapter 4
The New Rules of Selling

Rethinking the Sales Funnel

Is this 100-year-old model still relevant in the 21st century? Selling has changed from the 19th century, and most organizations and salespeople are stuck using processes and techniques that no longer work effectively. Consider the following:

When was the first sales manual produced?

1894, by the founder of the National Cash Register Company, John Patterson. He created a sales primer in 1887, then later developed a "Book of Arguments" and combined both into a sales manual.

When did the first sales funnel appear?

1898 by E. St. Elmo Lewis, who developed a model which mapped a theoretical customer journey from the moment a brand or product attracted consumer attention to the point of action or purchase.

When was the first catalogue direct-mailed?

1894 was the year Sears and Roebuck published its first catalogue.

What changed the game?

The internet changed "sales and marketing" to "marketing and sales."

The AIDA (Attention, Interest, Desire, Action) approach first appeared in print in 1903. This was the first time the sales funnel was explained. A few years before, something else was introduced that works like the sales funnel: the slot machine!

Early selling used one-way persuasion techniques focused on influencing the customer to take action in the direction which was in the best interest of the salesperson. It didn't matter if it was also in the genuine best interest of the customer.

The salesperson had all of the information and decided what information flowed to the customer. Limited information could be given to the customer as the salesperson saw fit and as best suited their needs.

It was accepted that sales is a numbers game, and large numbers of potential customers would go through the funnel to produce a much smaller number of prospects who would become paying customers.

The sales funnel model is an inward-looking, linear way of selling products and services. Now, think about the slot machine. It is an inward way of attempting to make money… just like the sales funnel.

It is a numbers game… just like the sales funnel. We keep putting money into it and watch the numbers narrow down and we either hit the jackpot or don't… just like the sales funnel.

The big payout happens occasionally; however, what keeps us playing are the small amounts of money we get while we are hoping for the big jackpot… just like the sales funnel.

The internet changed everything

The rules have changed. Information is available to everyone and no longer just to the salesperson. Clients want to do business with people they know, like, and trust. This is not "new news" – you already knew it. It's just common sense, yet it does not translate to common practice.

The key to success in the 21st century is to stop using your grandparents' sales techniques.

They don't work because people are more guarded than ever before and are much more informed than ever before.

It means you must move to attracting potential customers and clients to you and your business. This is not a nice-to-have… It is a must-have! Why? Because the rules have changed.

What are the new rules?

OLD RULES: Ask your potential customer what keeps them up at night.

NEW RULES: 90% of business buyers say that when they're ready to buy, they'll find you. (Source: Demand Gen Report)

OLD RULES: Say that you have the solution they need.

NEW RULES: 58% of buyers report that sales representatives are unable to answer their questions effectively. They want you to tell them something they don't know. (Source: Forbes Insight)

OLD RULES: Websites do not drive sales.

NEW RULES: If a buyer needs something, they will find you. 93% of business buyers use an internet search to begin the buying process. (Source: Marketo)

OLD RULES: The salesperson has all the information.

NEW RULES: As a salesperson, you no longer have an advantage over the buyer, because they have done their homework on the internet and may know more about your product or service than you do.

OLD RULES: 79% of marketing leads never convert into sales. Lack of lead nurturing is the common cause of this poor performance. (Source: Marketing Sherpa)

NEW RULES: Companies that excel at lead nurturing generate 50% more sales-ready leads at 33% lower cost.

OLD RULES: Use brochures and white papers.

NEW RULES: Use video. A recent IDG study reported that "64% of consumers have researched a product as a result of watching a tech-related video and close to half of them then looked for a product in a retail store (45%), visited a vendor website or contacted a vendor for information (45%), or purchased a product (44%)." The same IDG study goes on to explain how much digital is part of consumers' lives and that video is becoming the centerpiece of that consumer experience.

OLD RULES: Keep selling the same way and expect new results. 82.29% of salespeople say they don't have a consultative sales process or are not following the one they have.

NEW RULES: Companies that use a consultative sales process have more sales and happier customers. When asked, their customers said this about those salespeople: "They communicate that their firm knows my business, knows my problems, and knows how to solve my problems."

OLD RULES: The Elevator Pitch. Customers don't want to be pitched! The idea is to pitch yourself, in hopes of making a connection. A connection that could open a new business relationship. What worked in the past isn't guaranteed to work in the future. Human behavior has changed.

NEW RULES: When they ask, "What do you do for a living?" Instead of saying, "I'm a financial planner," say this: "I teach people how to save money," or, "I help people sleep better at night." Doesn't this sound more interesting while also begging the question, "How do you do that"?

OLD RULES: ABC – Always Be Closing.

NEW RULES: Don't pressure potential customers to buy. Be a problem solver, not a product pusher. Remember they're thinking, "I don't want to be sold to." Have a good understanding of their situation, then sit down with them and lay out a detailed solution. Show them how it's worked before.

OLD RULES: What can you sell this person?

NEW RULES: How can you serve this person?

OLD RULES: Basic, informational websites.

NEW RULES: Mobile-friendly websites. There are currently 4 billion mobile phones in use globally. Consider this:

38

- 50% of local searches are carried out on mobile devices.

- 86% of mobile internet users are using their devices while watching TV.

- A third of Facebook's 700 million users are using Facebook Mobile.

- 50% of Twitter's 175 million users are using Twitter Mobile.

OLD RULES: Mouth-to-mouth referrals.

NEW RULES: Buyers never buy anything until they've read reviews online and consulted their social network.

What can you do to adapt to the new way of selling?

With these new rules in place, it's hard to break through and set yourself and your company apart from your competitors. That's why attracting people is so vital to your future success.

As they've said, if they want something, they'll come to you. So now is the time to develop and implement new strategies to make them want to come to you!

What to do next
Change your mind set to 21st century thinking.

Here is the first thing you need to know: the sales funnel is still relevant today. The difference is this: the sales funnel is used by your prospective client.

Think about this: what do we do when we have a problem we want solved?

- We get online and search. We are searching for SUSPECTS.
- Next, we evaluate the different companies or services we found on the internet and whittle the list down to a few. We are turning suspects into PROSPECTS.
- After this, we check in with social websites to find out what they say about the company's product and service. This is getting REFERRALS and recommendations.

- The final step is contacting the company and getting answers to our questions. If it goes well, we buy and become a CLIENT.

Here are four simple steps to stop pitching and start attracting:

1. Stop selling what you do and start selling what your client can get done.

Ask, "How can I CREATE value for this person?" instead of, "How can I EXTRACT value from this person?"

Follow this formula: $P+R=S$. Problem plus Result equals Solution.

What's the point of offering a solution when you do not know what the problem is or the specific result the customer is after? Ask more questions. Make fewer statements.

Be a problem solver, not a product pusher.

Once you understand the problem and how the result will be measured, you can prepare how your solution will close the gap.

2. Know how clients measure value.

"Value" is an overused term and customers roll their eyes when salespeople bring it up. So how do you measure value? Here is the formula:

$V=R-P$. Value equals Result minus Problem.

If you follow my first formula ($P+R=S$) then the customer will measure value when they get the result they were after because the problem was eliminated. If you do this for your customers, they will tell everyone they meet who has the same problem to come to you.

3. Use your smartphone and stop collecting business cards.

The reason we collect business cards is to collect leads, add them to our database, and follow up. The reality is, all these business cards make it into the big stack of business cards you have collected over time that sit in a drawer in your desk.

Their information rarely makes it into the database for follow-up. Let me introduce you how to do this with 21st-century technology.

There are three things we never leave home without:

1. Our keys
2. Our wallet or purse
3. Our smartphone

Let me give you example of how to get your prospect or customers to use their smartphone to enter their contact information into your database. Your prospect or customer gets an automatic follow-up response and – get this – they are happy to do it.

Here we go:

Would you like a FREE copy of my book Unleashing The Power of Consultative Selling: Selling the Way Your Customers Want to Buy…. Not the Way You Like to Sell? If you do here are the steps to take:

1. Take out your smartphone and text the word **"consultative"** to 33444.
2. You will receive this auto-reply message: Hello! Please reply with a text containing only your email address so we can send you everything we promised. Thanks!

3. Enter your email and send.
4. Next, the auto-reply: Thank you for opting in! Reply with STOP at any time to unsubscribe from these messages. For assistance, text HELP.
5. Check your email and confirm your subscription.
6. The next email you get is a link to download your free book.

Now, what just happened?

1. I offered you something of value – my book.
2. You sent your email via text using your smartphone.
3. Your email address automatically goes into my database.
4. You get an instant follow-up email with a link to download my book.

It is a win-win. You get a FREE book and I just got a lead.

Imagine using this approach at network meetings, conferences, seminars, or any event where people ask what you do. You can do the same thing by offering a free video, checklist, guide, or book, as a few examples. How many more leads do you think would you capture, save, and send automatic follow-ups to?

When I teach this to my clients, they turn their entire organization into a lead-collecting machine delivering the same consistent message. This is called SMS marketing and there are plenty of companies who can provide this service to you. I use Leadpages.net.

4. Adopt the new mindset.

When I ask salespeople in my workshops what their goal is and they say, "To make more money," I tell them, "Making money is against the law… it is also called counterfeiting." Only the government can make money.

Your goal is to make a difference in your client's life, helping them to solve their problem by getting the results they want by providing them with your solution.

Why should you change?

Remember this: when you change your mindset, you change your results!

Chapter 5
Selling the Way People Want to Buy

My intent in sharing my personal stories is to illustrate my decision-making process and how this relates both in my personal and professional life. I asked you to think of the decision-making processes you've made, in order to change from what you were doing to doing something different.

It is important for you to understand why you buy in order to understand how your clients buy. After all, you are a consumer as well. Remembering that you have this in common with your prospects and clients helps you build connections with them.

Have you ever said to someone (or has someone said to you), "If I were you, this is what I would do"? This statement is a lie. If I were actually you, I would do exactly what you did because I would have your belief system, parents, schooling, life experiences, and so on. So, what are they really saying? "If I were you, I would do what I'm telling you."

People have internal rules and we tend to project our judgments and beliefs on others. When faced with a given event or decision, each of us has an opinion about how others should react or behave. This is also the case with sales; your client has a belief about salespeople and you have a belief about the prospect.

What happens first?

1. You tell a client they have a problem; or
2. They know they have a problem before you show up.

Using the illustration of my own aforementioned problems – I knew I had these issues, and what I did was to delay doing something about them. The dreaded status quo bias. It wasn't until I finally decided I could no longer accept the pain emotionally that I decided to take action and change. What finally got me moving out of my comfort zone was an insight that made staying where I was uncomfortable. I bet that if you thought about times you've decided to change, you found the same to be true for you.

This means it isn't you telling a client or prospect they have a problem; they already know it. The real question is this: "Has the problem gotten bad enough to take action?" And this question becomes: "Have you started researching to find a solution to their problem?"

The power of the click

What do you do when you have a problem? You Google it. The ability to get information which in prior times cost thousands of dollars to obtain now can be yours with a simple click of the mouse for free. This means your prospect or client can become educated on availability, cost, recommendations, pros and cons, and so on.

We all agree that in the 21st century prospects and clients are highly educated about the market, industry, competing companies, and reviews; and some will call this research "doing their homework."

I see it a bit differently. They are looking online at suspects and qualifying them into prospects based on their criteria –not yours. Their process begins with the words they use to determine what to search for and continues with the specific results those search terms bring up.

This means your prospects are qualifying you and your competition based on information that is important to them long before they are contacting you. 53% of decision makers have eliminated a vendor from consideration based on information they did or did not find about an employee online (Kredible Research).

What happens is that they land on your website and read the content – more importantly, they view your videos. The numbers are in and it's confirmed that video is exponentially more powerful than the written word. According to Forrester Research's Dr. James McQuivey, *"a minute of video is worth 1.8 million words"(*How Video Will Take Over the World, 2008).

After they have developed their short list they will dig in for more information about your company and your solutions compared to the others they have qualified. 77% of B2B buyers said they only speak to a salesperson once they have performed independent research online (CEB).

Next, they will contact you and your competitors to discuss and perhaps meet face-to-face. 36% of buyers said they don't contact a sales representative until they have put together a short list of preferred vendors (Demand Gen).

The prospect, after meeting with their short list, will decide to move ahead and select a winner or not. If they cannot see a clear path, once again the dreaded status quo bias steps in. 65% of customers are lost because of indifference, not because of mistakes (Blender).

What do you do before meeting a prospect? Go online to build a picture of your potential client. Even more common than Facebook, the more business-focused network LinkedIn tops the list as the preferred platform for meeting preparation (64%), followed by the company website (63%), and Google (61%). A third (34%) are also turning to Twitter to gain insight into their prospects' likes and interests.

Guess what? Your prospects are doing the same thing. They are checking you out before meeting with you.

What the top salespeople do is they don't use a sales process to sell. They are using a buying process to understand and adapt to the prospect or client. Understanding this helps them to have a conversion conversation. This type of process helps the client go through the decision-making steps in their buying process. They help prioritize the client's problem and use their solution exclusively to solve it.

Most salespeople will begin their presentations talking about themselves, their company, their locations, their clients, their products, and their services, and then finally they ask their client what problem they have. Remember, salespeople are like tacos, and after hearing basically the same stuff with a different presentation and with a different price point, it is no wonder prospects have trouble making a decision.

Prospects are looking for a pitch with helpful insights – insights that can help them understand what they will lose if they do not take action. How do you measure an insight? When your prospect says, "I didn't know that!" That's the "Aha" experience.

46

What did it take me to move out my comfort zone? It was fear. It was bad, and then it got worse. This experience wakes up the lizard brain by breaking thought patterns and providing a new and improved pattern.

We know that the prospect has done their research; however, if you can't break the prospect's pattern, then how else are you going to land a client who's already in the "why should I change and why should I pick you" mind frame?

Let me give an example. If I were to tell you that what keeps CEOs up at night is access to top talent for their organization, would this be an insight, an **"Aha"** moment? No, because you're telling me what I already know.

What if instead I said, "The most important job a board of directors will do is hire the CEO, and they are wanting to know a candidate's track record in decision-making accuracy over the span of their career." What we have discovered, through asking top-level executives across the country and across industries, is that the majority of executives answer between low 80% to mid 90% – otherwise they probably wouldn't be sitting in that seat. **What has been your experience?**

The next topic for the candidate is, *"Over the span of your career what has been your hiring accuracy?"* The same top-level executives tell us 50/50 or 60/40 at best. What has been your experience?

Hiring is a coin flip, yet making the wrong decision takes up valuable time, lost revenues, and employees leaving because of whom they report to, not because of the job or company; it gets even worse as morale suffers and your personal brand equity is at stake, leading up to your decision making being questioned. If this continues, you cannot regain lost time.

Does this example lead you to want to know what to do next? The insight I meant to communicate is to think about your hiring accuracy and realize it's a coin flip, a 50/50 outcome. For a decision maker, a hiring manager, this familiar risk often leads to problems and potentially a lot of trouble to them unless they do something different. This is an "Aha" moment for many people.

Listening with a Purpose

Nineteen centuries ago, Epictetus said, *"Nature gave men one tongue but two ears that we may hear twice as much as we speak."* Good advice then and good advice today. 80% of salespeople have a false belief that talking is the key skill of their profession. The top 20% know different. They know that listening is much more important. Ask the clients of the top sales performers and you will hear over and over again this comment: "They listen to me."

My sales representatives would take me out on sales calls and, before we got to the client's site, I would turn to my salesperson and ask, *"Why are we here?"* They would become like a deer in headlights... frozen. Their responses would be all over the place, but the bottom line was they had no specific plan, purpose, or outcome.

My next observation was their poor listening skills. No question about it, they could talk; but it was difficult to get them to stop. Sometimes, I had to break in to give the client an opportunity to respond to a question or to just talk to us, because of our limited time with them.

I always liked to have an immediate feedback session with that member of my team after we met with a client, so I proceeded to ask:

- What did our client just tell us?
- What did we learn?
- What could we do better next time?
- What did we do well?

This becomes an opportunity for coaching and reviewing our next steps. Listening more and talking less becomes a mantra.

Imagine for a moment there was a contest to meet and interview a famous celebrity in business, sports, television, movies, or public office – whoever it might be in your mind. You have just been contacted, informing you that you won!

This famous person, whom you admire, has granted you an interview. How exciting is this? But it is not over yet, because you will be a guest on Oprah to talk about it. You only have 30 minutes with this person and will not get another chance. Will you just show up? Or will you prepare in advance?

I bet you'll do your homework first to find out all you can. You will focus on which questions you will ask and perhaps think about what others might want to know, or what is important to them, or you might come up with a theme. Will you rehearse and practice the questions or will you just show up, keep your head down, and read from your papers?

The big moment has arrived and you make sure to bring your tape recorder to the interview. Why do you do this? So that you can recall what is said, because you do not want to miss anything important. Why do that? In preparing for the Oprah show, you will again want to prepare.

During the interview, you sit down and place your tape recorder on the table, push play, and record. You ask your insightful questions and, based on the responses, you ask other questions. The interview is a success!

Here is what you will NOT do:

- Take up most of the 30 minutes with you talking
- Interrupt them
- Answer the questions before they did
- Pause the tape recorder so you could talk about yourself

Or will you?

Changing your mindset to consider each prospect and client a *"celebrity"* and worthy of your time is not wasting their time. It is making each moment memorable. What do want your prospect of clients to say about you when you are gone? Because it will happen – they will talk about you.

Are you missing (the) communication? Think about your answers to these qualifier questions.

1. Do you spend more time talking than listening?

Many salespeople begin their presentations talking about their company, their clients, their products and services, and themselves before they ever give the prospect a chance to speak. Worse yet is, your prospects don't care. Is this you?

They want to talk about their problems and concerns, not yours.

2. Do you come up with a response in your head before they finish speaking?

I ask this question in my workshops: "How many of you talk to yourself? Raise your hand if you do." I usually do not see many hands out there. Then I ask, "Raise your hands if you think other people talk to themselves?" and I tell them, "Well, isn't this interesting! You all do."

Guess what? We all talk to ourselves, and that is okay. Somewhere along the way, talking to yourself gets to be a bad thing and, taken to an extreme, it can be. But the truth is, we all do it; and, yes, we even have arguments with ourselves.

Many times, this happens to a salesperson because they have been conditioned to believe that they must get their canned pitch said as quickly as possible. It happens automatically, like your brain is on cruise control as you wait for your client to take a breath so you can jump in.

However, the problem is that while you have a valuable moment to find out details of a problem within your prospect's mind, you are inside your own. Overcoming this mistake means suspending your judgment during the conversation and, when you're done, bringing back your judgments.

3. Do you jump in and finish their questions?

We sometimes put on our magic hat and become mind readers. We finish someone's thoughts and even interrupt to show you how good we are. We know more about what people need than they do and we give our advice freely.

We hate for the other person to pause, but we have adjusted, because we will just have another committee meeting. We will mind-read what others are thinking and tell them the right answer. Many of us do this and never realize it is going on, but this could be the reason your prospect never calls you back.

4. Do you ask so many questions that the client or prospect does not have time to think and answer them?

When doing this, the salesperson is not paying attention to what is happening in the mind of the person they are communicating with. Rapport has broken down. Through this mistake salespeople fail to recognize what's needed to get into rapport with the prospect and how to fix it once it is broken.

Getting into listening mode

A cat's whiskers are extremely sensitive, as they are closely connected to their nervous system. Whiskers give cats extraordinarily detailed information about their surroundings. They use messages from their whiskers to sense the presence, size, and shape of obstacles without seeing or touching them. Interestingly, whiskers also help cats smell odors. Okay, you are asking, "What do cat whiskers have to do with listening?" Lots! To be totally in a "record" mode, you must have your senses tuned up a notch and be aware of the person or people you are talking to.

You as a tape recorder is the metaphor I'll use to paint a positive picture of an interview scenario with your client or prospect.

Here are the steps:

Why am I here?

There are two questions you must answer. First, "What is your intended outcome for having this meeting?" Second, "How will you know if the outcome was met?" Many times, my sales staff would come back and report they had a "good meeting." I would ask, "What is the next step?" They might say, "We set up another meeting." "To do what?" Rarely would I ever receive a good answer to my last question. You see, the point of a meeting isn't another meeting. It is advancing the sale for some specific outcome.

Rapport

We use what I call "common sense language." When we communicate we use our senses, and our language reflects this by using seeing, hearing, or feeling words.

What happens if two people are speaking in different languages? Stuff is coming out of your mouth but the intent is missed. This is what miscommunication is all about.

- I told you this was important to my company.
- I never saw any of that in our meetings.
- I did not understand how strongly you felt about that.

If your client makes one of these statements, would you record it or not even register it?

We communicate to each other in different languages without realizing it. No wonder it becomes difficult to really get the intent of each other's communication.

Listen to find out which language or channel the other person prefers. Test your assumption to see if you are right. If not, ask a different question or find out how they feel about your discussion.

Take Notes

Before you take out your pad and pen, ask for permission first. Do not take so many notes that you are looking at your pad more than at your client.

Push Record

Metaphorically think of yourself as pushing a record button and be interested in the same way you would be with the famous celebrity.

- Do your homework

52

- Be interested
- Be respectful
- Be in rapport

What to do next

The difference in the way they buy forces a selling change. However, you already have a sales process. Can you still use it? Now is the time to access it. Is it 19th-century based or 20th-century based?

- Does it assume buyers are not knowledgeable?
- Does it promote an *"always be closing"* culture?
- Is it a sales process or a buyer process?
- Is it about winning a sale or helping clients solve problems?
- Does it ignore the power of the internet?
- Does it address the impact of social sites?
- Does it teach the importance of personal branding?
- Does it teach asking 20 questions?

Begin looking at your sales process and figuring out what your core sales message is. Where is the gap between what the prospect believes today and what they need to believe to buy your product or service? An example: there is a reason for those "before" and "after" pictures. Before losing weight and after. Before painting your car and after.

Most companies show you the "after" picture. For example, financial planners might use images of a happy elderly couple in front of the Eiffel Tower in Paris or on a sailboat. This is what you will get if you use my service, they say; but this tactic moves prospects toward the status quo rather than toward getting a retirement plan. Why? Because it lacks the *"before"* image – the pain of not taking action. So, first offer a path to fix the broken pattern by suggesting that your proposal addresses the fact that it's time for a change, before you go into "pick me instead of them" or propose your solution.

Clients expect more than just "sales training" in the people who meet with them. We are all familiar with typical sales training. Some focus on the basics and some more advanced. They are necessary, but are they sufficient?

Research shows us the sales skills which actually make a difference – that is, the difference in the client's decision to buy. They come from clients' rating of salespeople they interact with and those they have made repeat purchases with.

Only three sales skills made a difference:

- Personally managing the total client relationship
- Understanding the client's business
- Acting as a client advocate to correct any and all problems

What was the number one complaint? *"Didn't try to understand my business."* The most powerful training focuses on learning the client's business and reframing the client's thinking so that the salesperson can sell value and differentiate their product or service with insights and stories.

Chapter 6
The Ugly Truth About the Quota

We all know that in sales, quota is the most important thing that is discussed, reviewed, and depended upon, yet is misunderstood and rarely achieved as designed. Salespeople are measured on it, sales managers are measured on it, and even CEOs are measured on it.

Think about how the typical organization reaches quota. Annually the organization leadership meets to review the progress on strategic projects, financials, competitive situation, HR, and of course sales.

During the meeting, the discussion comes to setting quota and either the CEO, VP of sales, or the board comes up with a sales target which is known to every salesperson as "the Number."

How is the number, or quota, developed? The strategic plan – the financials plus the sales review – brings the CEO to declare the sales target. If the target is $20,000,000, the next step is to divide this number by the number of salespeople. If there are ten sales reps, then the number is $2,000,000 each.

A sales quota is a target for sales reps set for the month, quarter, and year by sales leadership. If you are a rep, you want to make quota and if you managing a sales team, you want to reach quota. Yet 67% of all sales people miss their quota, according to a recent study from The TAS Group.

The key is learning from past behavior to influence future outcomes. How many of the reps on your team achieved quota last year? What was the percent year over year growth? The historical performance of your individual sales team members versus quota is an important consideration to make when establishing sales goals. In addition, you should understand why some individuals achieved quota and why others fell short.

Sales quotas do nothing to help a salesperson or manager determine how much time or effort to put into what they do. A CRM or a data sheet filled with numbers doesn't show how a sales representative builds rapport or communicates value or generates business.

The data only shows the financial results of the salesperson's activity; so is it an accurate picture of the salesperson's level of performance? Worse yet, the data which management focuses on are the pipeline numbers plus their closes. These are all lag indicators, because you are looking at what happened, not what will happen. It does little good to discuss or even coach from this perspective.

To be effective, you need leading indicators that help you coach or understand what is happening in the early stages of sales. Coaching is much more effective on what your salespeople are doing at the beginning of the sales lifecycle as opposed to when they are closing their sales.

Quota are numbers on a piece of paper. What is the true measurement? It is sales productivity.

In fact, the #1 challenge for nearly 65% of B2B organizations is sales productivity, according to research from The Bridge Group.

Optimizing sales productivity is one of the most important aspects for a sales organization to focus on – the efficiency, effectiveness, and productivity of the salesforce has a direct and significant impact on revenue.

What is sales productivity?

Sales productivity is maximizing sales results while minimizing the cost, effort, and time. It's about the 20/60/20 rule. 20% of your sales team are top performers who often meet or exceed quota. 60%, which is the majority of your sales team, is your best bet for improvement and an opportunity to increase productivity. The bottom 20% should be moved to another part of the organization.

Since the 20/60/20 rule exists and 67% of salespeople don't meet quota, it comes down to how quota is determined. Quota is calculated with a simple math formula of taking the total expected revenue divided by the number of reps. This creates an average for each rep. To have an average means people will be above and below it.

Yet if we look at the 20/60/20 rule it is easy to see the greatest number of wins comes from 20% of the salesforce (often it is 10%). The question is, do you need to manage 3 different quotas? If the largest population of the salesforce is 60% to 70%, what is their average compared to the top group? What about the 20% of low performers? 10% should not be on your team and the remaining 10% are maybe on the right team – but not in the right role.

Where to focus?

The top sales performers tend to be the same one's year after year. What do they need? Support. Give them what they require and help them to do what they love to do. They already have a selling mindset and the traits of a top sales performer. Like any top performer, they are humble and always open for more coaching and learning.

Many sales leaders will want to help the 20% of low performers to become better performers. This is noble; however, when push comes to shove the real opportunity is with the 60% to 70%.

If quota is not the true indicator of sales performance, then what is? Once again, we turn to the top sales performers who consistently beat their quota successfully year after year. What is their secret?

It turns out it really is not a secret after all. It's sales productivity, and here are the three things they do.

They have a plan. Companies have plans, and so do individual top performers. Companies have financial objectives, growth objectives, and rewards incentives like increased market shares, bonuses, stock, and so on; so do these top performers. They have personal financial objectives, client targets, and personal and professional improvement objectives.

They know their numbers. Companies are tracking their numbers to understand if they are on track to achieve the company's objectives. Top performers do the same. They know the numbers needed in each stage of the funnel to achieve their sales goals. They know their conversion rates and trends and take corrective action.

They have a daily routine. What separates highly successful people from the rest? In part, it is their daily routine. They set up time each day for prospecting, meetings, advancing deals, and closing deals. I can walk in their office at a certain time of day and most often I know which of these activities they are working on.

Do a search online for *"daily routine of successful people"* and you will find thousands of articles giving you tips on what they do. **Why so many routines?** Because they work. How effective is sticking to a simple yet powerful daily routine?

Consider the daily routine Benjamin Franklin followed. He was one of our nation's Founding Fathers and held the titles of civic activist, author, political theorist, scientist, statesman, diplomat, and inventor. Among his many accomplishments, some of the most notable are: invention of bifocals, establishment of the University of Pennsylvania, discovery of lightning as electricity, the first mapping of the Gulf Stream, the first idea for Daylight Savings – and he was one of the five men who drafted the Declaration of Independence. That is a lot of achievement for an 8-hour work day!

How did his schedule help him do all of these things? It was simple and focused. And the most critical part is that he asked himself daily, *"What good shall I do today?"* He focused his mindset on a direction.

His schedule was structured for a routine. It also allowed for all the variables that each day's unique tasks and priorities brought. He had only six blocks of time scheduled each day:

- Getting ready for the day: shower, breakfast, personal study, and prepare for work (3 hours)
- Morning work (4 hours)
- Review of current projects and lunch (2 hours)

- Afternoon work (4 hours)
- Dinner and rest and wrapping up the day (4 hours)
- Sleep (7 hours)

So, simple, yet still structured, helpful and productive.

Many people resist the idea of structure or routine or a schedule. I used to be among them. But in truth, a routine like Ben Franklin's is extremely empowering. Once I began using this approach I found myself feeling good at the end of the day about what I accomplished and about myself.

There's no good reason a salesperson should live without any sort of routine, discipline, or accountability. Time management is a myth. You cannot go back to yesterday or last week and get your time back. What you control is not time but what you do with it. The secret to all of this is found in your daily routines and habits.

Think about how quota is created. It is a formula, and then the leadership guesses on what percent will make quota. Now I am not suggesting to abandon having a company goal and target. But would happen if salespeople set their own quotas according to their personal pipeline conversion number, goals, and abilities, and then those personal goals were rolled up into the company goal? Here's the thing: this is exactly what the top sales performers do and the rest do not.

What to do next?

What is quota really? When you think about it, what is the purpose of having a quota? What does it accomplish? In my experience, leading sales teams and working with clients, this is how I define it:

Quotas are goals. Quotas don't drive goals. Goals drive quotas. In developing their annual plans a company is really creating their business, financial, productivity, and profitability goals.

To achieve their goals a company takes clients, and when it solves their problems, the company receives money in exchange. To achieve the company's goals takes money, and this becomes quotas. Why? Because quotas are goals.

Each salesperson who succeeds has something in common. They have goals. Those who fail do not.

Salespeople must develop their personal goals and translate them into professional objectives, and sales leaders must help them to do this. Then they must provide coaching to help the salespeople achieve these professional objectives, and thereby they will also achieve their personal goals.

Goals solve problems. Why have a quota at all? Companies are faced with problems daily. There are competitive pressures to improve your service or products, not to mention to create and introduce new ones. Failing to do this is means losing clients (or not gaining clients). Increasing the top line revenue number and increasing profits is a constant concern. Creating financial and personal wealth for shareholders and stakeholders is of vital importance, though challenging.

Leadership continues to work on plans and tactics to solve problems through goal setting.

To put it simply, why have goals? To solve problems. The key is prioritizing the problems and then developing the goals that will address them.

Salespeople must look at their own selling mindset, skills, knowledge, and list of problems or challenges. Next they must prioritize them for the greatest return, not for what is easiest to do. Then, list the steps and time frames in which to do it.

Sales leaders must review their list and help not only with the priority; they must also provide assistance in solving the rest of the list as well.

Results eliminate problems. What is the little secret behind the boardroom doors? The discussion and focus goes to one thing. What is it? Results. It's what we all want, no matter our role in business or life.

The question is, what problems are facing us that we want solved? Once we take the steps to solve them, the evidence that it has been eliminated is determined by the results we see.

In leading sales teams and teaching sales professionals, I teach them a formula. It's already popped up in this book. P+R=S. Problem plus result equals solution. What's the point of offering a solution if you don't know what the problem is or the result the client wants? This is the failure of salespeople who sell a solution in hopes of finding someone with the problem.

Salespeople must look at what problems they must solve and if they do, what is the specific desired result. To say *"make more money"* is too vague. What problem will be eliminated and how much money will it take and what will you need to do to achieve it?

Measure eliminates argument. Every organization tracks their finances daily, weekly, monthly, quarterly, and annually. CRMs are designed to track each stage of the pipeline to monitor progress. The question sales leaders get asked is, "Will we make the number this quota?" CRMs are tools to provide reports that offer insights into whether they will or not.

You can argue about the market, competition, or product or services, but as one CFO told me, *"The numbers don't lie."*

At one point, I was teaching a sales team and I asked what their goals were. One rep said he wanted to retire early. I asked, *"How early?"* He replied, *"When I'm fifty."* I then probed a little deeper and asked, *"How much will you need to retire at fifty?"* The answer was, *"I don't know."* I gave him a dollar and wished him luck.

He had no way of measuring how much specifically he needed. What are his chances of meeting his goal without measuring it? We all know the answer. It is the same way with a quota. It's not an annual number divided by 12, or broken down further to a daily number.

You must know your personal conversion rates for each stage of the funnel. Once you know the numbers, you must review this every day to know which stage of the funnel to focus on. Is it leads, advancing, closing? If you say all of them, then this means none of them. If you push all your deals forward and close them and ignored filling in the top of funnel, you miss your number next quarter. Why? Because measurement eliminates argument.

Salespeople must know their personal pipeline conversions and numbers needed in each stage of the funnel. Every day you must review it to decide where to focus on that day.

Sales leaders cannot solely rely on CRM reports. They tell you what happened, not what will happen. Coaching begins with how to improve professional effectiveness at each stage to succeed, and this is best done weekly at minimum.

If you're a sales leader looking to lead and coach a consistent quota-crushing sales team, be looking for and coaching salespeople who are motivated by improving, not by accolades and awards. Going to the President's Club is awesome, yet the guy who is driven by making that trip isn't going to be your best rep.

Who is then? It's the one who has read all the sales books out there. They know and subscribe to the best sales blogs. They can tell you what their learning and mastery goals are. Their desire to get better and to learn is obvious.

Don't just measure performance goals, but incorporate mastery goals into performance reviews and coaching. Let the team know that you're not just measuring their ability to make quota, but also their ability to become a better salesperson.

Focusing on quota isn't the only indicator of sales success, in spite of what we've been led to believe. A commitment to focus on improving yourself, mastering the craft, and always learning – that's the secret to consistently making quota. Now the secret's out. It's the ***"Selling Mindset."***

Chapter 7
Coaching a Quota-Crushing, High-Performance Sales Team

Sales leaders and managers spend most of their time, energy, and resources on two groups of salespeople: their top performers and their worst performers.

The best reps are typically seeking coaching. That is why they are the best. They continue to improve their professional effectiveness. And sales leaders and managers like to spend time with them. They're proof of success. And they want to keep them happy so they don't leave for a different company.

The sales manager also spends time with their low performers because they demand attention. Or do they? The manager feels responsible for their results; they either need to coach them or let them go. Instinctively the sales manager knows this, yet he often decides to work with them to help them, and this only benefits a few –certainly not the ones who deserve your time.

And who doesn't get attention? The middle 60%. These salespeople have the greatest gain to make to hit or exceed quota. The top salespeople already are exceeding quota and the low-performing reps can take 80% of your available coaching time for little gains.

What is the difference between a ski instructor, a tennis coach, and a mentor?

A ski instructor teaches you the basics, from equipment, language, safety, basic skills, how to stop, how to get up, to much more.

When you have a tennis coach, you already have the basic skills. The coach is finding the weakness in your game and giving you specific instruction to improve your skills in order to help you improve your ability to win.

A mentor's role is to help you find the spark within to excel in your performance. They hold up a mirror to show you that what you are capable of is inside of you.

Which one is sales coaching? All three, depending on the who, what, when, and why. Are sales leaders and managers prepared to fill this role?

Let's face it, nobody I've ever met told their parents when they were a little kid, *"Mom, Dad, when I grow up I'm going to be a salesperson."* We got into sales by accident. There are a number of ways it happens. We got really good at what we did. We became the top salesperson, and then comes the promotion to sales manager.

The real world of the sales manager is the focus of senior leadership on them to report numbers. Quota is their top priority, even when the top priority for improving numbers should be improving productivity. They end up creating pivot tables, reports, and analysis, all to improve the accuracy of the forecast. At the end of the day these forecasts and spreadsheets have made no great impact in actually achieving the numbers.

There are many influences and conditions you cannot control that can affect that final number. For example, the economy, the weather, the competition... Yet, there is one condition you can influence, and it is your sales team.

As sales leaders and executives there is this misunderstanding of motivation. There is a false belief that you and I can motivate people to change from what they are doing to doing something different. The truth is, only you motivate you.

Yes, we are right back to the selling mindset, and what we do when we are selling is the same as for when we are coaching. We are asking salespeople to change something they are doing now to doing something different. And what I know about change is we don't like to change.

The good news is that you know how we change and how to use your knowledge in coaching your salespeople to greater success. You also know the processes that work and don't work.

Quota is asking every person on the team to meet the same sales goals. Taking the total revenue goal and dividing it by the number of salespeople is the easiest way to determine the quota. However, not everyone is capable of achieving at the same level. Some salespeople are better with a certain product or service; others work best with a certain type of client. You just can't get away from these complicated variables.

In one of the companies of which I'm the CEO, I have salespeople who are great at the transaction level. They are motivated by the hunt and landing the deal and going on to the next. They are not interested in building a long-term relationship. On the other hand, I have salespeople who love the relationship building and gaining more business from the same client.

I must coach the ones who like to knock on new doors differently than those who knock on the same door. Their numbers are not the same, meaning it is not one big number divided equally.

Your business is powerfully impacted by all these variables, and often coaching turns into asking the rep to ponder the question of whether or not they will make quota. This is not a choice, it is a dilemma. Instead of asking this question, master the art of flexibility by working with your salespeople. Discuss what's expected of them in order to keep the business growing. Each person must be evaluated based on their skills, knowledge, and interests.

The company sets annual revenue and profit company goals with plans so you all know what you're trying to achieve. The plans identify how their focus will serve your clients, shareholders, and employees. The CEO and everyone in leadership understands the importance to the plan to achieve the goals both personally and professionally.

Conventional wisdom dictates that it's critical to let your salespeople in on your company goal so they can understand where they fit into your plans. The goal is alignment – and this is where the conventional wisdom falls apart for most.

Why? Because this is logical, and we do not think logically. As you know, the lizard brain must get involved to communicate back and forth to the new brain, and ultimately the lizard brain decides.

What to do next

If you have company goals that are meaningful to you, I'm glad they are meaningful to you. It has been the company's objective to communicate its goals to the sales team so they will commit to meeting them.

The problem is alignment. There are some that will understand and believe in the organization's plan and others not so much. Imagine if you saw a salesperson's personal plan for success. Would you be likely to commit to it, and how would you align yourself to their attainment of their objectives? Not once or monthly, but weekly and daily? How difficult would it be? Yet isn't this basically what you are asking the salesperson to do?

Do you think the salesperson is more aligned with their own goals or the company's**?**

The best coaches work with their people to understand their current issues and jointly review what is working and what is not as they develop an action plan to achieve sales objectives. The question is, are they succeeding compared to **what?** Compared to the company's goals or their own?

You must have your salespeople develop their own personal sales plan that incorporates their personal and professional objectives. Next, they need to develop what specific actions they can take to improve their productivity. Your job is to ask questions to help them frame the issues holding them back and provide not just constructive feedback regarding how to improve, but also suggest specific actions for them to take.

There are many generic coaching models for this, yet they will fail you in the "selling" coaching session. They miss what's needed in driving the sales behaviors that will make the greatest difference.

Let's face it, many coaching conversations are deal-focused. CRM systems are great, but they provide information about what has happened, not what's going to happen. Coaching is about how to improve in specific areas, and this is when the sales manager must decide whether they are an instructor, a coach, or a mentor. Each has a place and each need to be tapped into when working with salespeople. The desired outcome is having them commit to their belief that their goal is achievable.

Do you believe, as many salespeople do, that sales leaders spend way too much obsessing over the numbers? How often do you hear or ask the questions "When is that deal going to close?" or "When are we going to get the contract?" or "When is that order coming in?" or "What is the invoicing status?" It's too late when deals are close to closing. How much can be done at this point? This is not coaching, it is simply about the numbers.

There is no question that the numbers are important; however, do not spend your entire coaching session focusing on this one area. Instead, shift your focus equally to early-stage deals. Good sales leaders are able to determine where the greatest impacts can be identified in the sales cycle process and pipeline to bring the greatest return. This results in greater sales productivity and performance for the salesperson, which is what helps you achieve your goals as a sales leader.

There is no silver bullet when it comes to sales coaching. However, when you focus and align yourself with your salesperson's personal and professional goals, you have a ringside seat to helping someone else to achieve what at one time they didn't believe could happen. When it does, that is the payoff.

Chapter 8
The Selling Mindset

The most important software you have to succeed in sales is not an app or on the cloud; it's not something you can buy. It is your mindset. One of the single most contributing factors of an individual's success can be traced back to this one factor.

A mindset is a set of beliefs that dictate what you and others should do when faced with an event. The event can be in business or life. When faced with an event, your decision to do or not to do is based on your beliefs, which are founded on your background, parents, education, friends, training, and so on.

Using my own personal experiences, I find I can summarize how I view an event in three simple yet powerful ways. This helped me with my own success and I use them in my programs. I've coined them *"The ABCs of Success."* Here is what they are:

Attitude is an outward expression of an inward belief.

Beliefs enable or disable my actions.

Communication is what I tell myself I can or cannot do.

Think about each one and I'm sure you'll agree how each one can affect our mindset. My goal in this book is to offer you a new mindset. One that will offer you some new things to consider in taking your selling skills to another level.

To show you what I mean about the power of a mindset, we will explore without judgment how to lose at sales and how to win at sales. To illustrate what I mean, I'll use a metaphor. Is success just the discovery of the recipe of sales?

Think of it this way. I live in the South where BBQ is king. Let's say you ask for the recipe for my BBQ sauce. If I were to give you the ingredients, you would not be able to duplicate my recipe because I did not tell you how much of each to use. If I gave you the ingredients and told you how much, you still could not duplicate it because I did not tell you the sequence of adding them. Once I give the entire recipe and you follow it, then you can get the same results.

We all follow a recipe of how we sell. We start your conversation the same way, ask the same type of questions, and follow the same steps to get a sale. This is how we as humans function.

I have a certain spot at home where I leave my car keys. If they are not there, it can't be that I put them somewhere else, so I accuse my wife of moving them. She of course says she didn't touch them. I always find them as I remember I had put them somewhere else (not my wife).

We all have steps we follow in the software called our mind. Like in the example with my keys – my mind automatically assumes they always are in a certain place. My mindset is such that if they are not there, then it couldn't have been me, it had to have been someone else who moved them.

The bottom line of this chapter is: when you change your mindset, you will change your results.

I'm Not in Sales

I will show you how this impacts your selling mindset by asking you what you think about being called a salesperson – is it negative or positive, in your mind? Are you proud of what you do or do you call your role something you are not?

In many companies, no one wants to be perceived as a salesperson. Over the years I've been given countless business cards by salespeople who attend my seminars and workshops or meet with me in one of the businesses I lead.

I have seen a pattern in these business cards that move away from the words *"sales," "sales representative,"* or *"sales executive."* Look at the business cards you receive and you will see sales representatives using titles such as *"customer service representative," "account executive," "customer satisfaction representative," "vice president," "area manager,"* or any one of dozens of other vague, misleading, fuzzy, or disingenuous titles.

The most popular seems to be *"consultant."* When companies rename their salespeople as consultants, there is no real change in what the salesperson is expected to do. Yet, a consultant's role is very different than a salesperson.

Does a salesperson need expertise to advise a client like a consultant does? The answer is yes –however, this ends once the sale is done.

A consultant has a very different outcome to deliver. Does a consultant need to sell? The answer is yes. The difference is, once the consultant gets the sale then their work begins.

So why would a company change their sales force titles to "consultant"? Because the company hopes to gain access to a prospective client organization's key decision makers. **Why?** The hope is that decision makers will view them as experts with the title of consultant versus sales representative.

Companies can spend an enormous amount of money converting their business cards, websites, and presentations to changes the word *"salesperson"* to *"consultant."* The question is, does this work?

Here's what happens. The consultant hands their business card to the receptionist and they read it and calls the person they have an appointment with and say, "The sales rep is here to see you."

People are not fooled simply by a title on a business card. Selling is a person to person relationship. If your mindset tells you not to identify yourself as sales and instead to call yourself something else, like a consultant, your hope that this misnomer will magically open doors to decision makers is like looking through a telescope from the wrong end. A title on a business card does not define who you are.

Using my metaphor of a recipe, let's look at some of the ingredients, or patterns, of what we find in unsuccessful salespeople.

72

Poor listening skills. They spend far too much time talking, and nowhere near enough time listening to what the customer truly wants.

Inability to identify client needs. They try to pressure the client to close the deal instead of building up the value of whatever it is they're selling.

Lack of follow-up. It's amazing how many times sales reps just give up after only one or two follow-ups to a lead or a prospect to whom they've already pitched. They don't hit their numbers and are doing themselves and their sales careers a huge disservice.

Lack of sufficient effort. They complain that the leads aren't any good, the market is tough, or the comp plan changed, making it too hard.

Not setting daily goals. Every salesperson has a sales goal that's set by the company. But they do not set achievable daily or weekly goals for themselves in order to achieve their quota.

Not knowing their numbers. If you want to close a certain number of deals per month, it will take measurable daily activity to get there: prospecting, calling, pitching, and following up. They don't get in the habit of setting smaller actionable goals, and do not come anywhere near hitting the bigger ones.

Failure to focus on top priorities. To succeed in any industry, you absolutely have to understand your product and/or service inside and out, as well as what your competition is offering that you aren't, and what you're offering that they're not, plus the market. Unsuccessful salespeople fail to understand what their clients' priorities are, and, combined with not looking at what is occurring in their segment, meet with failures.

Bottom line: They don't embrace being a salesperson. Possibly the biggest reason why some people don't last long in sales or fail at sales is they never embrace their profession. The general perception is people don't value salespeople as much as they should. They fall into the trap that this is true of every salesperson, causing them to take on this self-limiting belief.

You may have interacted with salespeople who have these traits. Every Salesforce has some of them. My advice to my clients is this: these people may be on the right bus; however, they are in the wrong seat.

What Top Sales Performers Do Differently

The best salespeople embrace their position and own it, understanding the role they play for their companies and their families. To put it simply, the best salespeople's mindset is that they love what they do.

Read the following statement and ask yourself how strongly you agree with it: ***"At work, I get to do what I do best every day."***

Gallup researchers found how you answer this question is one of the single most important questions they have ever asked. What did they find?

A person's answer links directly to their productivity, profitability, and customer loyalty measures. The more someone agrees with the statement, the better their performance.

Just doing more of what you do best can dramatically improve your performance. For salespeople, this truly means being on the right bus and in the right seat.

What can we learn from the patterns of highly successful salespeople? Let's examine some of the ingredients in their recipe.

They crush their sales goals. These reps are focused on attaining their goals and vigilant about tracking their progress.

Empathy. Empathy is the ability to place oneself in someone else's shoes. If a sales rep is selling something, they need to be able to feel the client's need and focus on finding ways for the product to meet that need if possible.

Self-motivation. They have a "fire in the belly" combined with self-discipline. It takes a highly motivated person to get up every morning and start making calls, planning and organizing their day.

Their road to sales success requires just that: the discipline to execute a well-organized plan. The most successful salespeople are self-motivated –it's what keeps them on their road of success.

Self-improvement. They are focused on improving their skills and knowledge. The best sales people I know are continually working to get a little better on knowing their market, clients, competition, and selling skills. They have humility because while they know they are really good, they are always open to getting a little better. Because they have this mindset of refining what they do or know and actively seek ways to get more efficient, they are and will remain top sales performers.

They ask the best questions. The best salespeople ask the best questions, and this is one of the reasons they win. They find out before they meet with a prospect or client what problems they may be or are facing and offer insightful and actionable information to help solve these problems.

They demonstrate the value of their product or service. They know how to create value with each client and prospect. Price is not the only motivating buying factor. Top salespeople know price is a factor in every sale but they also know that it is not always the primary reason someone makes their decision.

Top-performing salespeople keep in touch with their clients. They know that regular contact helps keep clients, so they send thank you, birthday, and anniversary cards. They make phone calls and schedule regular meetings. They send articles of value to their clients and are constantly looking for new and creative ways to keep their name in their clients' minds.

Think of the top salespeople you have met. What traits and patterns do they have? What would your list look like? Would it include some or most of the above, plus other attributes?

Remember my recipe example. If you know the ingredients, quantities, and the sequence, and you follow it, then you can get the same results as the recipe originally intended. People do not come out of the womb and get immediately diagnosed as a top salesperson or CEO or cook as the doctor spanks their bottom for the first time.

Why do geese fly south for the winter? Because they are geese. They don't know any better, they just do it. Only human beings can decide to go in any direction they choose. Anyone in sales can develop these traits. It takes effort, energy, and discipline but the end result can be worth it, especially when you consider how much more money top-performing salespeople make compared to the average salesperson.

What to do next

For many, the decision to change our mindset is a crossroad. You can continue staying on the same path as you are now on and get the same result. Or you can take a different path, one step at a time, to a new and better way.

We know there are no overnight successes. It takes time, and yes, there will be setbacks. You will learn from them and continue to get a little better.

The key is not getting 100% better tomorrow, it is getting 1% better each day. If you remain stuck with your current mindset, then anything you read from this point on are just words. Yet, if you decide to make small incremental changes, the words trigger a growth mindset.

Remember what I said earlier.

Attitude is an outward expression of an inward belief. If you do not have the mindset of a top sales performer, it will not matter if your company has outstanding products, services, and competitive prices. You still won't be able to sell very much. If you do not have this powerful mindset, you can read all the books on sales techniques and go to seminar after seminar and you will still never achieve the level of success you deserve. However, when you develop the sales success mindset, you will crush your quota and be well on your way to becoming financially successful.

One of the key reasons limiting the success of many salespeople is the lack of ability

To persuade another person to take action. Salespeople have been brainwashed into believing that sales and persuasion is bad. If this is your belief system, it has affected you and your success.

The sales success mindset is being honest with yourself and others. Your business card does not have to identify you as a sales professional or a sales executive, but you must be honest with yourself that you are a sales professional. Top sales performers know that they are sales professionals. This may seem obvious, yet it is not so obvious when salespeople have business cards saying they are something else.

Don't just blame your product or service for slow sales or rush to attribute a sales slump to high prices or some other factor outside yourself. Take responsibility. Empower yourself. Is anyone else selling more than you are selling given the same products, services, and prices? If so, what is the mindset of that individual?

When you take on the mindset of a top sales performer, you have tremendous energy to sell. You will have real enthusiasm, not phony, manufactured enthusiasm. With a powerful sales success mindset, you will love what you do. People will be drawn to you, your products, and

Your services. You will intuitively be able to persuasively describe all the benefits you, your products, and your services offer.

Beliefs enable or disable my actions. Do you want to know how to more persuasively describe the many benefits of the products and services you offer? The first and most important step is to develop a healthy belief toward persuasion and selling because if you don't, you will never use whatever sales and persuasion techniques you might know.

Thousands of books have been written on sales and sales techniques. You probably have a few, but how often do you read them? Do you ever use the techniques described? Why not? Is it because you will need to change, and this means taking action with a new mindset?

Communication is what I tell myself what I can or cannot do. I bet you have you read a book on selling in the past. Today you are probably not using the techniques you learned, or could have learned, from that book. **Why not?** There is probably a little voice in the back of your head saying, *"That's too hard," "It will take work," "I got by this far, why change?"* and *"I'm not that bad, I don't need it."*

Could the real reason that you don't hit your quota be that you're asking yourself, "What if I don't have what it takes to make it happen? What if I am not smart enough? What if I miss the goal and prove what others are thinking about me? What if I disappoint someone else? What if I let myself down?"

Thinking this way and telling ourselves these things is when fear sets in and in our brains, we feel the *"fight or flight"* dilemma. We avoid those goals even if we say we will try; the reality is that the fear is still there and it impacts our ability and willpower to change our thoughts and behaviors.

So how do I define sales? I think Dan Sullivan defined it best: "Getting people intellectually engaged in a future result that's GOOD for THEM, and getting them to emotionally commit to take action to achieve that result."

> **Bottom line:** When you change your mindset, you change your results. What will you decide?

Chapter 9
The "Crush Your Quota" Blueprint

The following are the action steps to take in order to consistently crush your quota as an individual salesperson or as a sales leader of a team. It begins with adopting DAC.

What is DAC? DAC is a strategy I use with my clients. It stands for Decisions, Actions, and Choices.

Decide. This is the first step you must undertake. You must decide that you wish to make a change in your life. No matter what it is, a firm decision needs to be made.

Action. Making a decision is not good enough; you must then take action. Action can be writing down an idea, making that call, or talking to people about your idea. Until you take action, nothing will happen. It is best to take action sooner rather than later. Those who procrastinate will wait and wait and wait.

Consequences. Every time you do something there are consequences. Always consider the consequences to see how they can affect your business and personal life, both in the positive and negative sense. Is going out with the guys for a few beers a good idea or will it cloud your judgment the next day? Will not making that call today be a really good idea?

Every choice we make causes change. By the way, remove the word "failure" from your language set. There's now only feedback.

Too many people fear what we call failure, however if you reframe the word and think of it as feedback and a way of learning from what has gone before, you will begin to learn and grow.

Everything you do can help you grow if you see it in the context of feedback rather than failure.

The Selling Mindset

Decide. What do you stand for? Is what you do helping your clients to improve their personal and professional effectiveness in meeting their needs, wants, and desires, and those of the people they serve? If it is, then it is your obligation to help them to achieve what they wish to.

You can change what you are doing, or you can change your mind set about why you are doing it. Both are achievable; however, one of them has a better payoff.

Action. What is your personal brand? Write down the answer to this question. Imagine your picture was hanging on a wall. What do you stand for?

- What would be the slogan underneath the picture say?
- What would you want to be known for?
- What do people say about you when you leave the room?

Complete this sentence: *"I'm known to my clients and peers as a person who [action words] and [result words]."*

Consequences. Answer the following questions:

1. What will happen if I choose not to make these changes?
2. What will happen if I make the changes?
3. I choose to make these changes because….

Personal Sales Plan

Decide. Doing the same thing and expecting a different result just because the quota number is increased is how people define insanity. Having an idea of what you want to do is not a plan, and it is not actionable. Decide not to leave your success to chance. Decide to write it down.

Action. We want the company to succeed and we want the company to complete the plans in growing the business and serving clients. Quotas solve goals. Remember, the lizard brain is looking after ME to move you to action.

Step 1 – Identify your personal goals first

- Write down your personal goals.
- Prioritize your list.
- Determine your top 1 to 3 goals.
- Write down what you will get when you achieve or exceed quota.

To determine where you are going, you first have to see where you have been, and this is the:

Step 2 – Perform a SWOT analysis

The purpose of the personal SWOT analysis is to identify actions you can take to best meet the requirements of a top sales performer or a high-performing sales team. Comparing your strengths and weaknesses will identify gaps and help you prepare to build your plan.

Perform a SWOT analysis. This is where the SWOT stands for:

- S = Strengths (internal)
- W = Weaknesses (internal)
- = Opportunities (external)
- T = Threats (external)

This process captures information about your internal strengths and weaknesses as well as external opportunities and threats. The key is to view your role as a salesperson as a business and yourself as a competitive product.

Strengths

To help you understand your strengths, picture yourself as a competitive product in your marketplace. A personal strength is an asset to you as a product and can be used as a way to differentiate yourself from others when you are building pipelines, communicating with clients, and closing deals. Examples of strengths: strong project management skills, ability to improve or reengineer processes, experience and training in presenting to large audiences, or proven successful sales abilities.

Weaknesses

A personal weakness is a liability or an area of opportunity for growth. These are characteristics you could improve upon to increase your communication with clients and number of wins. Examples: disorganized, uncomfortable speaking in front of groups, a tendency to procrastinate, or poor listener.

Opportunities & Threats

When thinking about your opportunities and threats, begin with the threats. Do this by comparing yourself to people you'll likely compete against for that next win or client as well as to the many reasons for "no decision." Then, as objectively as possible, judge your threats and determine possible ways to overcome them. Here are some examples:

Threat: Losing way too many deals because of "no decision."

Opportunity: Understand change and the status quo bias.

Threat: Sales processes are not effective in some areas.

Opportunity: Review processes and update them to be highly effective.

Step 3 - Set your goals

Some questions to ask yourself are:

- What problems do we solve and for whom?
- How can I add the six motivators to my presentation?
- Who are my best clients?
- What are the characteristics of my best clients?
- Where did most of my sales come from?
- Where do we want my sales to come from?

- What are some external/internal factors that can impact my sales (e.g., industry trends, technology, competition, business environment, etc.)?

Your goals should be SMART (Specific, Measurable, Attainable, Relevant, Time-bound).

Step 4 - Develop the sales plan

This is your map, and it is critical in helping you to arrive at the destination of achieving your goals. It will outline all the strategies and tactics you will use to overcome the obstacles or detours you may face along the way.

A strategy is a plan or map with the actions designed to achieve a particular goal. Developing sales strategies means writing down the risks or obstacles that you see in the way of achieving your goals, then write down some ideas on how you can overcome them. These include internal and external factors.

Tactics are short-term actions to help you execute your strategy. Tactics have clear deliverables and outputs using people, tools, and time and have minimal risk. When determining your tactics, write down the steps to achieve your milestones to execute and support your strategy.

Step 5 - Execute your strategy

Action speaks louder than words. Now that you have taken the time to plan out your map, it's time to begin the journey and act on it. The sales profession is one of the few professions where you can control how much you make or don't make by the actions you do or do not take. The plan is to help take away the risks of not beating your numbers and to achieve your personal and professional goals.

Step 6 - Evaluate and review planning processes

The world and your market are constantly evolving. If you write a plan and only look at it at the end of each year, that's like looking in a rear-view mirror instead of looking in the direction of where you are going. Just as important as writing the plan, it's important to:

- Review the plan monthly and quarterly in review meetings.
- Review what went well and what did not, and make adjustments weekly.

Consequences. While there are many reasons why salespeople may not have met their goals, the underlying theme comes down to a few critical factors:

1. No clear written goals
2. No plan written on how to achieve them
3. Failure to commit or take action on the plan
4. Not setting goals that are realistic

A sales plan is a crucial tool in helping you succeed in sales. Writing down a plan makes it a reality and helps you to identify risks and formulate a map, destination, and signs. It helps you to benchmark where you are at and where you want to go, so that you can make adjustments to achieve your goals.

Measurement eliminates argument.

Decide. Your sales plan is your map to success. Your numbers are the signs letting you know you are heading in the right direction. The signs are showing you know how far you've come and how far to go to reach your destination of beating quota.

Action. Know the number and percentages within your funnel of suspects, prospects, qualifying, closing, etc., in order to win deals. Know the average deal size in revenue.

Do the math and take your quota, increase it, and beat it by 15% or more. Take the total revenue and divide by the average deal size to determine the number of wins you need for the year. Using your percentages and determine the number you need in each stage.

Divide the numbers by 12 to give you a monthly number and divide by 4 to give yourself your weekly goals and then by 5 to give you a daily goal.

Consequences. Not knowing your numbers means you will fail.

Daily Plan

Decide. Yesterday is gone and tomorrow is not here yet. What you do today and in this moment, is the most important activity you will decide. Time management is a myth – you cannot go back and get your time refund. Decide to have a daily routine to work with your sales plan and supports your numbers.

Action. How do you accomplish what is needed each day to achieve your personal and professional goals and objectives? One person who accomplished a number of amazing, innovative achievement in many different roles was Benjamin Franklin.

How did he do it? He had a daily planner with a routine. He focused on whatever he had scheduled to direct his attention toward, which allowed him to maximize his efforts. Top sales performers do the same, and so should you.

Develop a routine for each day of the week. For example, emailing is best done early in the morning or late afternoon Tuesday through Thursday. Wednesday is when the majority of deals are closed.

Consequences. Showing up is not enough. It takes action to get your sales goals achieved. Unfocused action is time lost. And this is time that can never be regained.

Final Thought

Success is not normal. It is a choice. What do you choose?

I do not want to mislead you and tell you simply by reading this book you will win more sales. It will take hard work as does everything that is worthwhile in life. I've given you the tools to help you achieve more in your professional and personal life. Once you take what is here and apply it.

The key is don't try to do too much instead break it down into small manageable steps. It's not focusing on becoming a 100% better. It is becoming 1% better each week. This is the path to success.

Knowledge is power only when action is taken otherwise it is powerless. Do not be the type of person that continues to search for information. Be an action taker not an information seeker.

The good news it you do not need to do this alone. Join me and others in my private Facebook group Crush My Quota to get free training and support. And I will see you at the President's Club.

About the Author

Richard Grehalva is the CEO of three companies, a TEDx speaker, and a best-selling author whose works include Unleashing the Power of Consultative Selling, Crush My Quota, The Boomerprenur Revolution and Asking for Directions. His book Unleashing the Power of Consultative Selling is a required textbook in a graduate school of management.

Find out more about Richard at:

www.resultsnotadvice.com.

Resources

To work with me, visit www.resultsnotadvice.com, where you can view my programs and sign up for my free newsletter.

Join my private Facebook group, *"Crush My Quota,"* for FREE training and to connect with other like-minded professionals.

Would you like a FREE copy of my book Unleashing the Power of Consultative Selling: Selling the Way Your Customers Want to Buy…. Not the Way You Like to Sell? If you do, here are the steps to take:

1. Take out your smartphone and text the word *"consultative"* to **33444.**

2. You will receive this auto-reply message: **Hello!** Please reply with a text containing only your email address so we can send you everything we promised. **Thanks!**

3. Enter your email and send.

4. Next, the auto-reply: Thank you for opting in! Reply with STOP at any time to unsubscribe from these messages. For assistance, text HELP.

5. Check your email and confirm your subscription.

6. The next email you get is a link to download your free book.

Go to www.crushmyquotaplanner.com to get access to the first planner system designed specifically for salespeople and sales managers. The system contains the 3 things the top performers use to crush their quotas year after year.

References

Why We Buy: The Science of Shopping, Paco Underhill

IDG 2017 Customer Engagement Research Report.

Forrester Research's Dr. James McQuivey, "a minute of video is worth 1.8 million words" (How Video Will Take Over the World, 2008).

Sales Development 2018 METRICS and COMPENSATION Research report, The Bridge Group.

Neuromarketing: Understanding the "buy Button" in Your Customer's Brain

Book by Christophe Morin and Patrick Renvoise

www.ingramcontent.com/pod-product-compliance
Lightning Source LLC
Chambersburg PA
CBHW070943210326
41520CB00021B/7030